Black Bears

By Mara Grunbaum

Nature's CHILDREN™

Children's Press®

An Imprint of Scholastic Inc.

Content Consultant
Nikki Smith
Assistant Curator, North America and Polar Frontier
Columbus Zoo and Aquarium

Library of Congress Cataloging-in-Publication Data
Names: Grunbaum, Mara, author.
Title: Black bears/by Mara Grunbaum.
Description: New York, NY: Children's Press, an imprint of Scholastic Inc., [2019] | Series: Nature's children | Includes index.
Identifiers: LCCN 2018023395| ISBN 9780531127148 (library binding) | ISBN 9780531134269 (paperback)
Subjects: LCSH: Black bear—Juvenile literature.
Classification: LCC QL737.C27 G79 2019 | DDC 599.78/5—dc23

Design by Anna Tunick Tabachnik

Creative Direction: Judith E. Christ for Scholastic Inc.

Produced by Spooky Cheetah Press

Printed in Heshan, China   62

SCHOLASTIC, CHILDREN'S PRESS, NATURE'S CHILDREN™, and associated logos
are trademarks and/or registered trademarks of Scholastic Inc.

1 2 3 4 5 6 7 8 9 10 R 28 27 26 25 24 23 22 21 20 19

Scholastic Inc., 557 Broadway, New York, NY 10012.

Photographs ©: cover: Mark Raycroft/Minden Pictures; 1: Lynn_Bystrom/iStockphoto; 4 leaf silo and throughout: stockgraphicdesigns.com; 4 top: Jim McMahon/Mapman®; 5 child silo: All-Silhouettes.com; 5 bottom: John E Marriott/age fotostock; 5 bear silo: Viktorya170377/Shutterstock; 6 bear silo and throughout: nanovector/Shutterstock; 7: David Nunuk/Getty Images; 9: Dave King/Getty Images; 11: OSTILL/iStockphoto; 13: Matthias Breiter/Minden Pictures; 14: Michio Hoshino/Minden Pictures; 17 top left: jtyler/iStockphoto; 17 top right: Don Johnston/age fotostock; 17 bottom left: tuasiwatn/Shutterstock; 17 bottom right: topseller/Shutterstock; 18: Matthias Breiter/Minden Pictures; 21: Ingo Arndt/Minden Pictures; 23: Danita Delimont/Getty Images; 24: Mark Newman/Getty Images; 27: Suzi Eszterhas/Minden Pictures; 28: Peter Mather/Getty Images; 31: dssimages/iStockphoto; 33: The Print Collector/age fotostock; 34: Michael Leidel/EyeEm/Getty Images; 37: Jan Luit/Buitenbeeld/Minden Pictures; 38: Mark Raycroft/Minden Pictures; 41: Frans Lemmens/Getty Images; 42 center left: Eric Isselee/Shutterstock; 42 bottom: Mark Taylor/NPL/Minden Pictures; 42 center right: Sonsedskaya/Dreamstime; 42 top: GlobalP/iStockphoto; 43 top left: Natalia Volkova/Dreamstime; 43 top right: Alexchered/Dreamstime; 43 center: anankkml/iStockphoto; 43 bottom: Wolfgang Kaehler/age fotostock.

◀ **Cover image shows a black bear cub— already adept at climbing trees!**

Table of Contents

Fact File: Black Bears

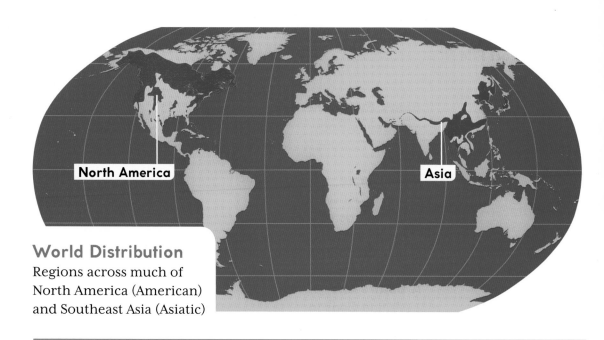

North America

Asia

World Distribution
Regions across much of
North America (American)
and Southeast Asia (Asiatic)

Habitat
Forested areas,
streams, swamps,
meadows, and
open tundra

Habits
Mostly solitary
except for mothers
and cubs; typically
spend the morning
and evening
looking for food
and rest at midday
and at night; in
colder areas, spend
winter in a
sleeplike state to
save energy

Diet
Mainly fruits,
berries, nuts, roots,
and stems; also
honey, fish, insects,
rodents, and
animal carcasses

Distinctive Features
Big bodies with
short, stocky legs;
short tails; curved
claws; small eyes,
round ears, and
long snouts

Fast Fact
Most black bears
in the wild live for
10 to 15 years.

Average Size

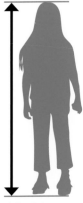

**4 ft. 6 in.
(1.4 m)**

5 ft. 6 in.
(1.7 m)

Human (age 10)

Black Bear (adult)

Classification

CLASS
Mammalia
(mammals)

ORDER
Carnivora
(tigers, bears, hyenas,
seals, related animals)

FAMILY
Ursidae
(bears)

GENUS
Ursus
(brown bears, black
bears, polar bears)

SPECIES
- *Ursus americanus*
  (American black bear)
- *Ursus thibetanus*
  (Asiatic black bear)

◄ A black bear eats
salmon in a part of
Canada known as the
Great Bear Rainforest.

CHAPTER 1

Bears Everywhere

It's a chilly fall morning in northern Wisconsin. The birds in the forest are starting to chirp and stretch their wings. High up in a tree, something furry starts moving. The tree branches begin to tremble as a 300-pound (136.1-kilogram) American black bear climbs down the trunk to the ground.

Black bears are the most common bears in North America. They can be found from the Alaskan tundra to the woods of Florida, and from Canada to northern Mexico. They make their home in at least 40 U.S. states. Their closest relatives, Asiatic black bears, live in Southeast Asia. There are more black bears alive today than all other species of bears combined.

American black bears often live close to humans. Sometimes they wander into places where people live. This can cause problems. But typically, black bears are peaceful animals that just want to keep to themselves.

▶ Black bears climb trees to feed, rest, and hide.

A Bear's Body

An adult black bear is about 3 feet (0.9 meters) tall and 6 ft. (1.8 m) long on all fours. When it's standing on its hind legs, this **mammal** can reach 7 ft. (2.1 m).

Black bears have short tails, small eyes, and round ears. Their noses and mouths form a pointed **snout**. A black bear has curved claws that it uses to tear apart food. The bears' claws also enable these animals to be excellent climbers. Unlike some animals, bears can't **retract** their claws. They scratch them on trees to keep them sharp.

A black bear's weight depends on its age and the season. A typical adult female weighs from 90 lb. (40.8 kg) to 250 lb. (113.4 kg). Males weigh from 130 lb. (59 kg) to 500 lb. (226.8 kg). That makes black bears the smallest of the three bear species in North America. Brown bears can weigh 1,000 lb. (453.6 kg) or more. Polar bears, the largest, can weigh more than 1,200 lb. (544.3 kg)!

Fast Fact
Black bears can walk on two legs but usually use all four.

Round Ears
swivel to allow
the bear to hear
in all directions.

Large Nose
gives the bear
a strong sense
of smell.

Thick Fur
keeps the bear
warm in winter.

Claws
are curved to
help the bear
climb trees and
rip open food.

Big Paws
press flat on
the ground to
support the
bear as it walks.

Close Cousins

Asiatic black bears, also called moon bears, are similar to American black bears. But the two species have some notable differences. For one, the Asian bears have a large white patch on their chests. This marking is sometimes shaped like a "V." Moon bears also have slightly smaller bodies than American black bears do. They weigh only about 220 lb. (99.8 kg) on average. Their ears are larger and farther apart than those of American bears. And the fur around their neck and shoulders is longer. Sometimes the fur looks like a ruffled collar!

The black bears of Asia live in **remote** areas. It can be hard for scientists to find the bears and observe them. That means that people don't know much about what the bears do in the wild. Instead they learn from bears living under human care in places like zoos.

▶ Asiatic black bears live in forests in China, Nepal, and other Asian countries.

CHAPTER 2

Living Wild

If you live in North America, chances are that black bears are living somewhere nearby. Black bears use many different **habitats**. Most live in forests. They also wander through meadows and across streams. Bears in Alaska and western Canada hunt along the coast. In the eastern United States, they live on mountains and in swamps.

A black bear's exact size, diet, and habits all depend on its location. The animals can adjust their lifestyle to help them survive wherever they are. The bears can even look different in different places. Despite their name, black bears aren't always black. Those that live farther west often have brown or reddish coats. Some in Alaska appear blue-gray. On the west coast of Canada, black bears are sometimes born with white fur! Just like humans, black bears in the same family can have different hair colors.

▶ About 400 black bears with white fur live in western Canada.

Fast Fact
Black bears
can run 30 mph
(48.3 km/h) for
short distances.

Super Senses

Because bears have small eyes, many people think they have bad vision. But that isn't true. Scientists think that black bears see at least as well as humans do. They also have good night vision.

A black bear's sense of smell is even better. The folded **membranes** inside its nose are 100 times as big as a human's. This allows the bear to sniff out food from more than a mile away. That's better than a bloodhound—a dog famous for its sense of smell!

But a bear can only smell things when it's facing toward them. It needs another way of knowing if danger approaches from behind. That's where its sharp sense of hearing comes in. A bear's ears can hear in all directions. They're about twice as sensitive as human ears. If a bear hears a person or another bear coming toward it, it quickly scampers away.

◀ A black bear's pointed canine teeth help it catch fish and other prey.

Hungry as a Bear

Black bears are big—and they have big appetites to match. These **omnivores** eat whatever they can find. Most of the time they're plant eaters. Their favorite foods are berries, nuts, grasses, stems, and roots. Occasionally, bears hunt insects, fish, or rodents. They don't kill bigger animals, but they may feed on dead animals they find.

A particular bear's diet depends on where it lives. In the Great Smoky Mountains, berries and nuts make up most of a black bear's meals. Asiatic black bears eat more meat. In Alaska, the bears eat shore grasses and hunt salmon from rivers. Sometimes they even feast on beached whales.

Black bears remember where they find meals. Unfortunately, bears that live near people may start eating human food. They find it at campsites, in garbage cans, or even inside homes. Storing food safely can help people in these areas avoid problems with bears.

▶ These are just a few of the many foods black bears may eat.

Wild Blueberries

► A single black bear can eat up to 30,000 berries a day.

Ant Broods

► Black bears dig up ant eggs in winter, when berries are scarce.

Whitebark Pinecones

► Bears can crack open the hard cones of pine trees to eat the nuts inside.

Sockeye Salmon

► Salmon swimming upstream in summer and fall give bears another source of food.

Dawn to Dusk

A black bear's day starts very early. It wakes up before sunrise to start **foraging** for food. The bear stays busy the whole morning. It might wander and eat for several hours before taking a break. During the middle of the day, the bear often rests. It naps on a soft spot on the ground or climbs up into a tree to snooze. Around sunset, the bear forages awhile. Then it settles down to sleep for the night.

As a bear forages, it helps the **ecosystem** around it. For example, the bear often tears apart rotting logs to look for insects. This helps break down the dead trees so new life can grow. The bear may also help spread new plants by eating berries. The tough seeds survive the trip through the bear's body. Then they come out in the bear's droppings and start growing in a new place. The pile of bear poop even provides fertilizer for the new plant!

◄ Napping in a tree helps a black bear avoid people and other bears.

The Big Sleep

When winter arrives, food often becomes scarce. Salmon rivers freeze. Berries rot away. But black bears have a way to survive this tough time. They find a cozy spot under a rock or in a hollow tree. Then they **hibernate**, or enter a sleeplike state.

As a bear hibernates, its body changes to save energy. The bear breathes less often. Its heartbeat slows down. Its body temperature drops from 100°F (37.8°C) to 90°F (32.2°C). Black bears in Asia get even colder. Their temperature plummets as low as 40°F (4.4°C)!

Black bears can spend up to seven months in hibernation. They don't eat, drink, or go to the bathroom the whole time. They lose up to 25 percent of their body weight. In spring when the bear eats again, these body changes are reversed.

Not all black bears hibernate. In warmer areas, a black bear may leave its **den** for an occasional snack. If enough food is available, the bear may stay active all year.

▶ Black bears gather leaves and twigs to use as soft bedding for their dens.

CHAPTER 3

A Bear's Life

Some mammals live in groups for protection from **predators**. But black bears are big and strong enough not to need that. Black bears are mostly **solitary** animals. Each has its own feeding **territory**. A male's territory can span up to 100 square miles (259 square kilometers). Female territories are smaller, at about 25 sq. mi. (64.7 sq km).

To mark their territories, the bears rub themselves on trees. This leaves their scent behind. They also use their claws to make long scratches on the bark. If another black bear sees or smells these markings, it knows to stay away. Sometimes the bears' territories overlap. Two bears may arrive at the same feeding site, such as a salmon stream. When this happens, they usually keep their distance and don't fight. But that changes in springtime, when bears come together to **mate**.

▶ A black bear scratches its back and leaves its scent on a birch tree.

Mating Season

There's one time of year when black bears meet on purpose. In late spring or early summer, they get together to mate. At this time, male bears may fight over a female. They stand on their hind legs and swat each other with their front paws. The stronger male gets to mate with the female bear.

The mating process lasts only a few days. Then the male and female bears go their separate ways. They have another big job ahead of them. In late summer and fall, bears stuff themselves with all the food they can find. They need to store up fat before they start hibernating. The biggest males can grow to 800 lb. (362.9 kg)!

By late fall, the black bears have eaten enough to last them all winter. They settle into separate dens to sleep.

◀ A male bear's sharp teeth and claws can leave permanent scars on his rival.

Born in Burrows

It's only after the pregnant female has settled into her den that the embryos inside her body start developing. About three months later, in January or February, she wakes up to give birth. A mother black bear can have anywhere from one to five cubs in a litter. But twins are the most common.

The newborn cubs are blind and helpless. They each weigh less than half a pound (0.2 kg). They haven't grown any fur yet. Their mother snuggles and breathes on them to keep them warm. She shifts her weight carefully to avoid hurting the tiny cubs.

As the female bear continues resting, the babies nurse and grow. Their mother's milk provides all the food they need. But the mother bear still isn't eating. Over the course of the winter, she can lose up to a third of her body weight. She'll have to leave the den to eat soon. Otherwise, she and her cubs won't survive.

▶ A mother bear licks her three-week-old cub to keep it clean.

Fast Fact
A black bear's
ears are the first
part of its body to
grow to full size.

Hello, World!

As spring approaches, the black bear's habitat warms up.
Plants start to grow. Fish return to streams. The cubs and
their mother emerge from their den in late March or early
April. The cubs are about two months old. It's the first
time in their lives that they've seen the outside world.

When they first leave the den, the cubs weigh about
5 lb. (2.3 kg). They still need their mother's protection
from predators like coyotes, bobcats, and bigger bears.
The female bear guards the cubs fiercely. She grunts and
charges at any predator that comes near.

The cubs keep nursing for another five months. Then
they start eating alongside their mother. By the time the
cub is one year old, it can weigh about 80 lb. (36.3 kg).
That's over 150 times as heavy as it was when it was born.
If a human baby grew at that rate, he or she would weigh
more than 1,000 lb. (453.6 kg) by preschool!

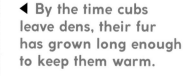

◀ By the time cubs
leave dens, their fur
has grown long enough
to keep them warm.

Young Explorers

Young black bear cubs have a lot to learn. Even after they've stopped nursing, they stick close to their mother. She shows them what to eat and where to find food. She watches as they practice climbing trees.

The family stays together while the cubs learn to fend for themselves. The young bears are curious and explore the world around them. They play with each other and with objects they find. In fall, they help their mother build a new den for winter. They hibernate alongside her one more time.

The next summer, the mother bear is ready to mate again. A female does so every other year. That means it's time for the young bears to strike out alone. Their mother chases them off to find their own territories. At 18 months old, they're ready for the adventure. In just a few years, they'll start mating and having cubs of their own.

▶ Cubs learn to climb by watching their mother.

CHAPTER 4

Ancient Beasts

The first bears lived in Asia about

27 million years ago. Scientists believe they were about the size of foxes. Over millions of years, the bears grew and spread around the world. In 1935, scientists found evidence of another bear, one that lived 2 million years ago. This giant animal, known as the short-faced bear, stood 11 ft. (3.4 m) tall on its hind legs. Its arm bone was almost as big as an elephant's!

American black bears first appeared around 5 million years ago. For a time, they shared the land with their gigantic short-faced relatives. But about 10,000 years ago, short-faced bears became **extinct**. Now black bears, brown bears, and polar bears are the only bears in North America.

▶ Ancient humans may have hunted cave bears, an extinct relative of black bears.

Bears of the World

Today there are eight bear species around the world, including American and Asiatic black bears. Bears live on four different continents. They make use of all kinds of habitats. Polar bears hunt seals on ice in the Arctic. Some brown bears live in the Asian desert of Mongolia, where they eat wild rhubarb plants.

All bears have some things in common. They have round ears, small eyes, and short tails. Their faces are pointed, and their feet press flat on the ground. They belong to a group of mammals called **carnivorans**, which have claws and sharp teeth to rip apart flesh. But not all bears use this ability. Giant pandas, for instance, live almost entirely on bamboo.

◄ Giant pandas are found in the wild only in certain areas of China.

CHAPTER 5

Sharing the Planet

Several bears have been hunted throughout human history. Now many of their habitats are under threat. Humans live near bears and build farms and houses in their territories. As a result, the **populations** of many bears are in decline. Unlike most of their relatives, however, American black bears are growing in number. About 900,000 live in North America today. Their ability to adjust to different habitats makes it easier for them to spread.

People are moving into black bears' habitats. That means human encounters are becoming more common. Most black bears find people scary. If they hear or smell a person coming, they'll likely run away. But bears that get used to human food can become less afraid of people. That can be dangerous for all involved.

▶ Black bears can find food in garbage cans, at campsites, and even in backyard bird feeders.

Human Conflict

Black bear attacks are extremely rare. In fact, humans pose much more danger to the bears than they do to us. Hunters kill black bears for their meat or fur. Drivers hit bears by accident. More bears die from these run-ins with humans than from natural causes.

If you see a black bear, don't approach it. Keep your distance and stay calm. Talk to the bear and wave your arms slowly. This tells the bear that you're a human, not **prey**. If the bear moves toward you, it's probably just curious. Don't run or climb a tree—it might chase you. Stand your ground and keep making noise. Clap or bang pots and pans together. Make yourself look as big as possible. When the bear stops moving, slowly back away.

If the bear does attack you, fight it. Kick it and swat it with your arms. Hit it with rocks or sticks. This should scare the bear away.

◀ This bear is curious about the hiker in its path, but the animal will soon run away.

The Future of Bears

Unlike American black bears, Asiatic black bears are declining in number. One reason is that **poachers** can make money selling bear parts. Some people in Southeast Asia use the bears' **bile** to treat disease. But scientists are working to help the animals. They have developed a human-made version of bear bile. They hope that this will help people rely less on the bears.

Scientists are trying to learn more about black bears. They want to know how the bears survive things that make people sick. People who gain too much weight can develop health problems. But bears stay healthy as they gain weight every year. Researchers are studying the bears' hibernation. What they learn could help doctors treat problems like **obesity** and heart disease.

People may never uncover all the black bear's secrets. But the more we know about the shy, lumbering animals, the easier it will be for bears and humans to coexist.

▶ Parts from Asian black bears are sold at an illegal market in Myanmar (Burma).

Black Bear Family Tree

Black bears are carnivorans—mammals with teeth and claws built to hunt. All carnivorans have a common ancestor that lived about 50 million years ago. This diagram shows how black bears are related to other carnivorans, such as raccoons, sea lions, and dogs. The closer together two animals are on the tree, the more similar they are.

Sea Lions
medium-sized carnivorans that have flippers for limbs and that hunt fish in the ocean

Raccoons
small, omnivorous carnivorans with nimble paws for climbing and grabbing food

Giant Pandas
large black-and-white bears that eat mostly bamboo and very little meat

Dogs
medium-sized carnivorans with strong muscles and teeth that can tear

Ancestor of all Carnivorans

Note: Animal photos are not to scale.

Polar Bears
very large, white bears that hunt seals on floating Arctic ice

Brown Bears
very large, omnivorous bears with large paws and long claws for digging up food

Asiatic Black Bears
medium-sized, omnivorous bears with black fur and a white chest patch

American Black Bears
medium-sized, omnivorous bears with a coat that can range from black to white

Words to Know

B .... **bile** *(BYLE)* a substance produced by an animal's body to help break down food

C .... **carnivorans** *(kahr-nuh-VOR-uhnz)* a group of mammals that have claws and sharp teeth for catching and ripping apart other animals; they may or may not depend on meat to survive

D .... **den** *(DEN)* the home of a wild animal

E .... **ecosystem** *(EE-koh-sis-tuhm)* all the living things in a place and their relation to their environment

embryos *(EM-bree-ohz)* the earliest forms of unborn humans or animals

extinct *(ik-STINGKT)* no longer found alive

F .... **foraging** *(FOR-ij-ing)* going in search of food

H.......... **habitats** *(HAB-i-tats)* the places where an animal or plant is usually found

hibernate *(HYE-bur-nayt)* when animals hibernate, they sleep for the entire winter; this protects them and helps them survive when the temperatures are cold and food is hard to find

L .... **litter** *(LIH-tuhr)* a group of offspring born to an animal at the same time

M.......... **mammal** *(MAM-uhl)* a warm-blooded animal that has hair or fur and usually gives birth to live babies; female mammals produce milk to feed their young

mate *(MAYT)* to come together to produce young

membranes *(MEHM-braynz)* thin, flexible layers that make up part of a plant or an animal

N .... **nurse** *(NURS)* drink milk from a breast

O .... **obesity** *(oh-BEE-sih-tee)* the condition of having too much fat in the body

omnivores *(AHM-nuh-vorz)* animals or people that eat both plants and meat

P .... **poachers** *(POHCH-uhrz)* people who hunt or fish illegally on someone else's property

populations *(pahp-yuh-LAY-shuhnz)* all members of a species living in a certain place

predators *(PRED-uh-tuhrs)* animals that live by hunting other animals for food

prey *(PRAY)* an animal that is hunted by another animal for food

R .... **remote** *(rih-MOTE)* far away from people or places where people live

retract *(REE-trakt)* pull back into the paw

S .... **snout** *(SNOUT)* the long front part of an animal's head, which includes the nose, mouth, and jaws

solitary *(SAH-li-ter-ee)* not requiring or without the companionship of others

species *(SPEE-sheez)* one of the groups into which animals and plants are divided; members of the same species can mate and have offspring

T .... **territory** *(TER-i-tor-ee)* an area that an animal or group of animals uses and defends

tundra *(TUHN-druh)* a type of land with permanently frozen soil and low-growing plants such as mosses and shrubs

Find Out More

BOOKS

- Gish, Melissa. *Black Bears* (Living Wild). Mankato, MN: The Creative Company, 2018.
- Jeffries, Joyce. *Black Bears* (Bears of the World). New York: PowerKids Press, 2017.
- Omoth, Tyler. *American Black Bears*. Mendota Heights, MN: Focus Readers, 2017.

WEB PAGES

- www.bear.org

  The North American Bear Center provides information about black bears' diets, adaptations, and behavior.

- www.nps.gov/subjects/bears/index.htm

  The U.S. National Park Service gives an overview of North American bear species and how they interact with humans.

- tracker.cci.fsu.edu/blackbear/about

  This site from Florida State University describes black bears' life cycle and how the animals relate to their environment.

Facts for Now

Visit this Scholastic Web site for more information on black bears:
www.factsfornow.scholastic.com Enter the keywords Black Bears

Index

Index (continued)

About the Author

Mara Grunbaum is a science writer who loves to learn about strange and fascinating animals. This is her fourth book for kids. She lives in Seattle, Washington, with her cat, Zadie, who sleeps almost as much as a bear.